Fine
KITCHENS
&
CABINETRY

TINA SKINNER

Schiffer Publishing Ltd

4880 Lower Valley Road, Atglen, Pa 19310

Schiffer Books are available at special discounts for bulk purchases for sales promotions or premiums. Special editions, including personalized covers, corporate imprints, and excerpts can be created in large quantities for special needs. For more information contact the publisher:

Published by Schiffer Publishing Ltd.
4880 Lower Valley Road
Atglen, PA 19310
Phone: (610) 593-1777; Fax: (610) 593-2002
E-mail: Info@schifferbooks.com

For the largest selection of fine reference books on this and related subjects, please visit our web site at **www.schifferbooks.com**
We are always looking for people to write books on new and related subjects. If you have an idea for a book please contact us at the above address.

This book may be purchased from the publisher.
Include $5.00 for shipping.
Please try your bookstore first.
You may write for a free catalog.

In Europe, Schiffer books are distributed by
Bushwood Books
6 Marksbury Ave.
Kew Gardens
Surrey TW9 4JF England
Phone: 44 (0) 20 8392-8585; Fax: 44 (0) 20 8392-9876
E-mail: info@bushwoodbooks.co.uk
Website: www.bushwoodbooks.co.uk
Free postage in the U.K., Europe; air mail at cost.

Designed by RoS
Type set in Huxley Vertical BT/Zurich BT

ISBN: 978-0-7643-3205-0
Printed in China

FOREWARD

There are many reasons why homeowners want a custom kitchen. For some it's about having the latest appliances, for some it's about having a showplace, and for some it's actually about cooking. No matter what the motivation, there is one common thread: We all want a special place to share good food and conversation with our family and friends – a place where we share our lives, a refuge from the ringing cell phone, hockey practice, and rush hour.

It seems we all end up in the kitchen. I know my family does. We have a beautiful dining room and a comfortable family room where our gatherings usually start out. But, we gravitate to the kitchen sometime through the evening. I'm not sure why; maybe it's the memory of family dinners while we were growing up; maybe it's because that's where the food we just enjoyed was lovingly prepared; or maybe it's just because it's a great space where everyone can be themselves and share commonalities we all have – food and laughter.

Christiana Cabinetry has become the realization of a dream I didn't know I had. I wanted to be a farmer like my dad, but thanks to a wonderful teacher who encouraged me to use my God-given talent, I learned to build. I started out in this business making furniture and followed a natural progression into cabinetry. It has been one of the most rewarding experiences of my life – especially when a new kitchen is installed and the homeowner sees it for the first time.

From the moment our clients begin talking to us about their wishes, wants, and needs for a space, we can see them dreaming of years of shared laughter, homework, frank conversations, and even a good practical joke now and then. These are the same things we want in our own kitchens and we take designing and building the perfect setting very seriously.

We understand that every homeowner has their own personality and style. That's why we offer over 100 door styles, 14 wood species, endless veneers, and 62 standard finish options – as well as the ability to craft unique door and molding designs and match just about any color, including the flower painted on Aunt Betty's favorite spaghetti bowl! These are the elements that make a space uniquely yours.

Christiana Cabinetry has an extensive network of designers throughout the United States, Canada, and Bermuda who, along with their client homeowners, have graciously shared their kitchens to make this book possible. Every kitchen you'll see was hand crafted by our artisans to capture the homeowner's wishes.

We are honored that you've invited Christiana Cabinetry into your home – whether it's to draw inspiration from our designs or to let us craft the cabinetry around which you'll share wonderful times with your family. And, I want to extend my appreciation to all of our clients already enjoying their kitchens – thank you for giving us one of the most amazing and rewarding journeys imaginable.

I wish incredible journeys for you as well.

My best regards,
Gerald Metzler

Contents

Introduction

From storage and work center to social center, the kitchen is the heart of your home. Because it is probably the room you spend the most time in, you want it to project your personality and style, yet be a work-friendly space. The one element that brings those things together is your cabinetry.

Kitchen cabinetry is the most visible and used part of any kitchen. It unites the other materials – countertops, appliances, flooring, fixtures, hardware – you are using. It's the canvas that allows you to show your style; the aspect that creates the personality and charm of the space.

Cabinetry is the largest investment and probably the most confusing of all of the decisions you'll make for your new kitchen. Here are ten tips that will make your project easier, more enjoyable and ensure you will have the space you desire.

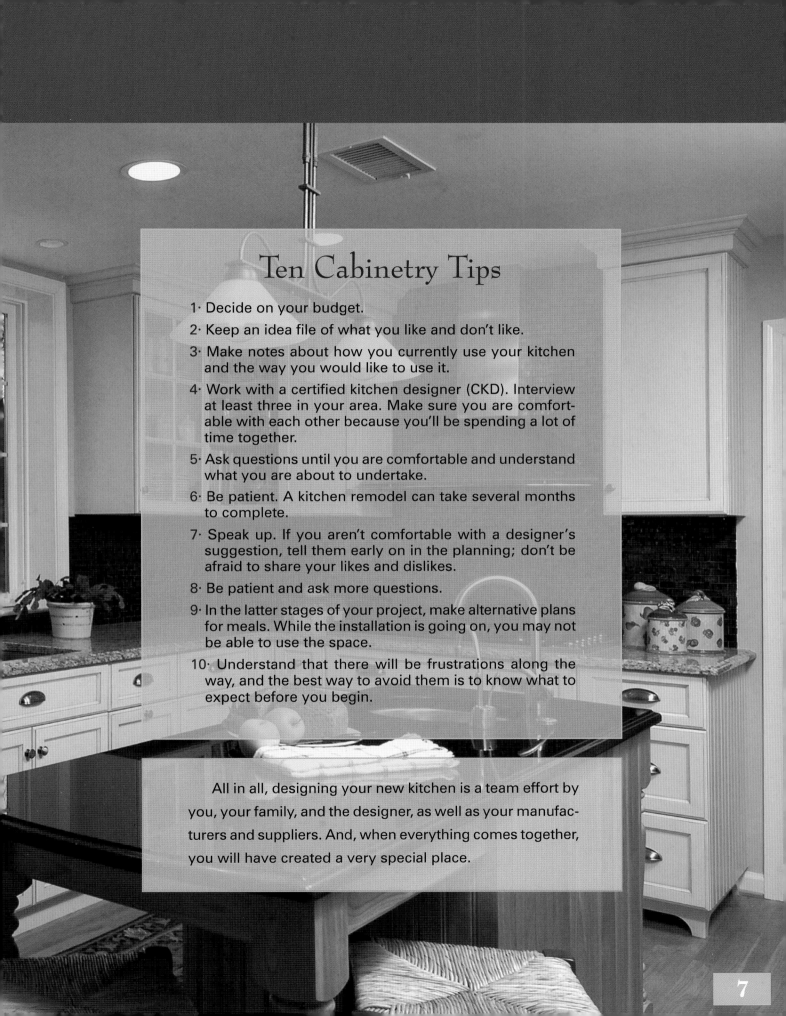

Ten Cabinetry Tips

1· Decide on your budget.

2· Keep an idea file of what you like and don't like.

3· Make notes about how you currently use your kitchen and the way you would like to use it.

4· Work with a certified kitchen designer (CKD). Interview at least three in your area. Make sure you are comfortable with each other because you'll be spending a lot of time together.

5· Ask questions until you are comfortable and understand what you are about to undertake.

6· Be patient. A kitchen remodel can take several months to complete.

7· Speak up. If you aren't comfortable with a designer's suggestion, tell them early on in the planning; don't be afraid to share your likes and dislikes.

8· Be patient and ask more questions.

9· In the latter stages of your project, make alternative plans for meals. While the installation is going on, you may not be able to use the space.

10· Understand that there will be frustrations along the way, and the best way to avoid them is to know what to expect before you begin.

All in all, designing your new kitchen is a team effort by you, your family, and the designer, as well as your manufacturers and suppliers. And, when everything comes together, you will have created a very special place.

KITCHEN COMPLIMENTS

The biggest trend in kitchen cabinetry today is the incorporation of individual pieces. These "cabinets" appear as fine furnishings within the home, and their beauty and design is custom created, both to stand out as an individual piece, and to compliment the overall kitchen design. Hutches, desks, islands, and tables alike are designed to embody individual "wow" factor for the kitchen, while integrating harmoniously with the room as a whole. A different finish, unique molding or embellishment, or the incorporation of metal or glass grids might set the piece apart, while some aspect, even if just the finishing glaze or the door pulls unites the piece with the rest of the room. You will see such pieces in kitchens throughout this book, but here, a few have been drawn forward to illustrate the concept.

Photographer: Bob Narod
Designer: Karen Hourigan, CKD, ASID

Custom cabinetry mimics antique hutch in this beautiful buffet unit.
Courtesy of Kitchen & Bath Studios

Photographer: Beth Alongi
Designer: Julie Stoner, CKD, ASID

A pretty built-in wine hutch features a curved front and wine
pockets below, mullioned glass display windows above.
Courtesy of Kitchen & Bath Galleria

PETITE

Small kitchens create the biggest challenge for kitchen designers. Consumers today want all the appliances to make their lives easier, and to help them create the increasingly sophisticated meals demanded by an evolving culture of cuisine. Yet, along with those double ovens, the dishwasher, microwave, double-wide fridge, and perhaps an espresso machine and a bun warmer, they also need a place to store the comestibles, cookware, condiments, and spices that accompany any food preparation task. Oh – and it has to look good, too.

When starting with a small architectural footprint, whether it's in a historic farmhouse or a city flat, a designer's first challenge is to squeeze in all the "necessaries," and then find clever ways to fit in the rest. Every year sees new innovations in ways to increase space usage in the kitchen. Clever designers and cabinetmakers have collaborated to claim more space in the back of the corner cabinet, to tip out drawers that tuck beneath the well of a sink, and ways to tuck work surfaces away when they're not needed. The following kitchens demonstrate wonderful ways to utilize space, both in terms of using it, and in the joy of decorating it.

Photographer: Charlie Smith of
Ft. Myers, Florida
Designer: Patti Miller

Small on space, this little condo kitchen is big on island style. Cabinets inset with woven jute make an artful statement, while a central island has been carefully carved to mimic bamboo. *Courtesy of PRO Interiors*

Photographer: Terry Roberts
Designer: Catherine Hodgins

A wall of cabinetry end with a pantry on the far end of a galley kitchen, preserving wall space for a bank of windows and a
stretch of island that make this relatively small cook space feel
wide open. *Courtesy of Kitchens by Design*

On the other end of the spectrum, kitchens have continued to expand in new home construction as builders respond to consumer demand. In remodels, kitchens tend to steal space from other rooms, encroaching on lesser-used spaces as homeowners claim more room for the place where they find themselves happiest – the hearth of the home.

Large islands have become the central gathering place in homes, where friends and family congregate during social occasions or for everyday meals. The open air atmosphere of today's kitchens, where the cook can look through to dining and living areas, has become the standard in-home design over the past decade. Homes lacking this amenity are likely to have interior walls moved to accommodate greater views from the kitchen.

This new aesthetic has had a huge influence on the way kitchens are designed. Firstly, the idea of a work-triangle was developed to help people negotiate their tasks in the unrestricted spaces these great kitchens created. Designers carefully thought out placement of refrigerator, sink, and cook centers to minimize the mileage on those preparing food. As the concept has evolved, the setting for these great kitchens has morphed to include banks of cabinetry that unify the expansive view, and furnishings that punctuate the great expanses. Home offices have moved into kitchens and, in some cases, laundry centers and entertainment areas, as well.

Where traditional homes had a separate kitchen, often next to a back door, and connected to the rest of the home only by a narrow doorway, most kitchens designed today are interconnected with every aspect of family life. Moreover, they are important showplaces and part of the proud fifty-cent tour for visitors.

Photographer: Taylor Photography
Designer: Bill Noval

A stainless steel hood vents the workstation atop a great central island. Wall cabinetry was all but banished from this kitchen to preserve the view outside. *Courtesy of Spyglass Design, Inc.*

15

Photographer: Terry Roberts
Designer: Catherine Hodgins

Arched windows provide an eye-catching backdrop for this coal-black kitchen. The room's octagonal shape is traced in wood in both ceiling and floor. Stainless steel appliances and a slab of artful glass countertop emphasize the room's contemporary feel, contrasted with an old-fashioned wood-fired oven outlined in an arch of brickwork. *Courtesy of Kitchens by Design*

Photographer: Terry Roberts
Designer: Catherine Hodgins

Wood countertop adds warmth to this classic gray kitchen, underlined by solid flagstone. A big work island plays center stage in this open floor plan. Globe lighting enhances the futuristic feel of the space, reflected off a high-gloss ceiling. *Courtesy of Kitchens by Design*

Photographer: Taylor Photography
Designer: Gayla Olson

Clerestory windows illuminate an
expanse of kitchen, open to a living
area beyond. Windows and all their
light are a wonderful aid in the ability to
admire this space, with its stunning tile
backsplash and warm terracotta floor.
Courtesy of Spyglass Design, Inc.

The biggest trend in home design today is a harkening back to the aesthetics and workmanship of yesteryear. Those seeking the very best have looked to the Old World for inspiration – to the kind of solid, hand-carved wood creations enjoyed by ancestors and treasured by generations. The earthy materials of wood, stucco, real stone, and hand-crafted tiles have brought a new richness into our lives, and a greater appreciation for our atmosphere. Moreover, today's consumer is trying to bring a bit of the lifestyle of the Old World home, where local traditions and close-knit families engendered leisurely meals, enjoyed late into August evenings. The kitchen embodies both the aesthetic of the surrounds and the setting for memory-making activities spent with those most important in our lives.

Photographer: Peter Rymwid
Designer: Peter Salerno, CMKBD

An entryway to a kitchen frames the elegant
room beyond, where a range-top surround
forms a fireplace-like focal point. *Courtesy of
Peter Salerno, Inc.*

Photographer: Peter Rymwid
Designer: Peter Salerno, CMKBD

A raised ceiling with backlit stained glass creates a sense of being in a garden conservatory. The kitchen has been outfitted with a pair of classic urns flanking the range, and a center island that evokes a centuries-old antique. *Courtesy of Peter Salerno, Inc.*

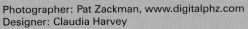
Photographer: Pat Zackman, www.digitalphz.com
Designer: Claudia Harvey

Immaculate detailing in carved wood, crafted tile, and elegant appointments make this a stunning kitchen. Stacked ovens and an enormous range are among the modern amenities, but the atmosphere is decidedly old world. *Courtesy of Claudia Harvey*

Photographer: Zack Benson Imagery
Designer: Heather Moe, Senior Designer

This kitchen feels like a step back in time to old Europe. Every element stands on its own unique merits in the room, the pieces fitting together like a great collection in a space furnished with faux marble columns, gorgeous mural work, and a coffered ceiling framed in layers of crown molding. *Courtesy of Kitchen DeBonaire*

Photographer: Beth Alongi
Designer: Julie Stoner, CKD, ASID

Antiqued cabinetry in buttermilk tones coordinates with the perfect marble countertop in this elegant kitchen. A recessed ceiling gives the room shape, while arched openings above windows and refrigerator add elegance. *Courtesy of Kitchen & Bath Galleria*

Photographer: Beth Alongi
Designer: Julie Stoner, CKD, ASID

A home office finds the perfect nook, at the center of action where the main hallway, dining areas, and kitchen converge. *Courtesy of Kitchen & Bath Galleria*

Photographer: Steven
Paul Whitsitt

A colorful sunflower
theme and elaborate
hand-carved details
make this kitchen
unique. *Courtesy of
Christiana Cabinetry*

31

Photographer: Peter Leach, peter-leachphotography.com
Designer: Nathan Eitner, Harve Cook

The design objectives for this rural Pennsylvania home were to provide a spacious, professional-quality kitchen that would serve as the social gathering place for the home. The low ceilings and linear space provided a design challenge. To maximize the beauty of the countryside, expansive windows and glass doors were installed. A dramatic, granite-topped island created functional counter space and storage. Fluted columns enhance the ceiling height, combined with graceful arches to reduce the linearity. *Courtesy of Chester County Kitchen and Bath*

The design of the kitchen
flows into office space.

Closer to home, the refined woodworking skills of Colonial craftsmen are being revived to furnish America's fine kitchens. Turned legs, scalloped skirts, and hand-oiled finishes are a coveted look in today's kitchen design world. The following kitchens explore this interesting evolution back to American roots.

Many embody the perfect simplicity of the Shaker craftsmen. None so perfected the simplicity of woodworking, and the beauty of furnishings, so poetically as the shakers. With purposeful intent and impeccable crafts-manship, this small, now defunct, American religious sect left a huge influence for future furniture designers to emulate. Their design legacy has never faded, and the look remains timeless, whether in a colonial home or a modern loft.

Photographer: Bob Narod
Designer: Jerry Weed, CKD

Charcoal tones in the glass tile backsplash, and a black-granite countertop on the central island add counterpoint to the antiqued white cabinetry. Stainless steel drawer pulls coordinate faucet hardware, appliances, and the range hood. Storage space has been maximized. *Courtesy of Kitchen & Bath Studios*

Photographer: Peter Rymwid
Designer: Joe Salerno, CKD

A large, arched doorway opens the kitchen to the rest of the home. Just beyond, a wet bar in matching cabinetry creates a secondary culinary center, where beverages are matched to cuisine. *Courtesy of Ribbon and Reed Cabinetry*

Photography: Zack Benson Imagery
Designer: Heather Moe, Senior Designer

Visible from the formal dining room and the library, this narrow, ugly kitchen provided walk-through access to a sunny, west-facing breakfast room. It lacked counter space and storage—but most of all, it lacked personality. Designer Heather Moe saw the kitchen as an opportunity to show-case the homeowner's extensive dinnerware collections and sunny personality. To address the issue of the formal adjoining rooms, visible and eye-catching areas such as the range/hood and sink area were designed to be charming as well as functional. The side of the range/hood area was enhanced with posts and a decorative panel end. This narrow, rectangular space turned out to be surprisingly functional when reconfigured as a true galley kitchen. Two long straight runs of cabinetry were installed and the ends of the room were used for separate furniture pieces. Distressed finishes and furniture styling added a sense of history; cheerful wallpaper, a pretty celery-green granite countertop, and the distinc-tive, sculptured pulls added personality. *Courtesy of Kitchen DeBonaire*

Photographer: Lisa Farrer
Designer: Susan Lund, AKBD

These clients requested Calcutta marble and pewter for their countertops. Because there were two different counter styles, the designers added two cabinet styles, a rich cherry finish on the wall and baseboard cabinets with an antiqued black island. *Courtesy of Spacial Design*

Photographer: Tom Thompson
Designer: Catherine Hodgins

A very approachable island offers all
sorts of angles for friends, family, and
helpers to step up, or pull up a chair. An
assortment of cabinetry creates a sense
of furnishings for the room, including two
built-in hutches finished in antique red.
Courtesy of Kitchens by Design

Photographer: Iesha Gomillion
Designer: Jerry Weed CKD

Handsome wood finishes add dignity and style to a space rich in storage. A long central island provides seating and the cook's research center, with useful appliances and storage stacked along the surrounding walls. *Courtesy of Kitchen & Bath Studios*

Photographer: Iesha Gomillion
Designer: Karen Hourigan, CKD
Builder: I.P. Construction

An angled peninsula adds interest and countertop to a galley kitchen. Classic cabinetry has been imbued with the patina of tradition, with beveled panels and crown molding. A second oven was placed under the counter to maintain counter space. A pantry area was created near the breakfast nook with two elegant floor-to-ceiling armoire units sandwiching a matching hutch. The left cabinet is a refrigerator, the center houses a TV on an arm, and the right cabinet holds a working desk close to the action. *Courtesy of Kitchen & Bath Studios*

Photographer: Iesha Gomillion
Designer: Fred Grenfell, CKD
Contractor: John Cassell

Crown molding and classic hardware give this kitchen its traditional feel, though the openness of the space and the expanse of the marble central island spring from modern-day sensibilities. *Courtesy of Kitchen & Bath Studios*

Photographer: Iesha Gomillion
Designer: Jerry Weed, CKD

A beautiful wood countertop sits center stage in a kitchen outfitted in warm, provincial colors. A bank of windows fills the space with sunlight, illuminating a wash station with a great porcelain farmer's sink at its heart. This kitchen is nicely plumbed with another wet sink on the island, and an elevated faucet over the cooktop. *Courtesy of Kitchen & Bath Studios*

Photogrpaher: Iesha Gomillion
Designer: Jerry Weed, CKD
Builder: Bowa Builders, Inc.

A black central island anchors this classic kitchen, crafted in earth tones from the wooden floor planks to the great stretches of beams overhead. A professional-quality cook center is at the heart of the kitchen, with a paneled hood overlooking an easy-to-clean tile backsplash in a multitude of earth tones. The cook's reference books are kept close at hand under the island. A bright window connects the kitchen to the outside, with potted plants close to their water source: a copper farmer's sink snug in the corner. A wet beverage station makes it easy to delegate the pleasurable task of decanting wine and serving cocktails. *Courtesy of Kitchen & Bath Studios*

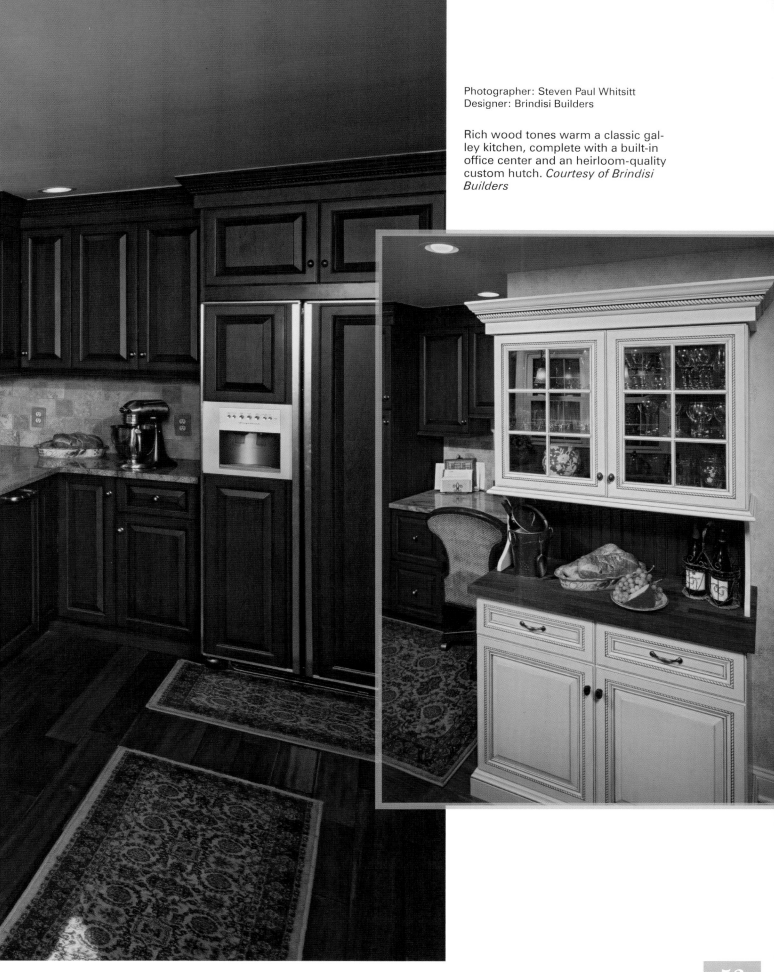

Photographer: Steven Paul Whitsitt
Designer: Brindisi Builders

Rich wood tones warm a classic galley kitchen, complete with a built-in office center and an heirloom-quality custom hutch. *Courtesy of Brindisi Builders*

Photographer: Steven Paul
Whitsitt
Designer: Brindisi Builders

The contrast between floor, white cabinetry, and painted walls adds energy to this room. The infusion of white brightens and heightens what was once a standard space. *Courtesy of Brindisi Builders*

Photographer: Steven Paul Whitsitt
Designer: Brindisi Builders

Rich tones unite a kitchen that has it
all. *Courtesy of Brindisi Builders*

Photographer: Joseph Kelly
Designer: Dot Taccarino

A corner workstation is an inherent part of any modern kitchen. Bills and recipes alike are kept close at hand, in electronic format.
Courtesy Asbury Kitchen and Bath

Photographer: Joseph Kelly
Designer: Dot Taccarino

Antique finishes on the cabinetry play in off-white tone to a rich burgundy backdrop. The cook center takes center stage, a mantel above the cooktop caps a tile backsplash crafted from marble.
Courtesy Asbury Kitchen and Bath

Right:
Photographer: Joseph Kelly
Designer: Dot Taccarino

A central island provides workspace, and an elevated area becomes a buffet when the leaded glass doors to the dining area are opened. *Courtesy Asbury Kitchen and Bath*

Photographer: Joseph Kelly
Designer: Dot Taccarino

A window seat serves as a breakfast nook and contemplation corner on the far side of the island. *Courtesy Asbury Kitchen and Bath*

Photography: Pat Zackman, www.digitalphz.com
Designer: Claudia Harvey

A classic Tudor home in need of an updated kitchen but with limited space called for maximizing every inch of the room. The clients were in desperate need for storage as well as modern amenities. The original kitchen felt closed in and dark. To open up the space the ovens were moved to the back wall and cabinets were wrapped around the corner, creating additional counter space. The island was downsized so as not to overpower the room, but to be a functional home to an under-counter refrigerator, trash compactor, and prep sink. In keeping with the Tudor style, a dark finish was chosen for the cabinets, but lighted by using a lighter countertop, backsplash, and flooring.
Courtesy of Claudia Harvey

Photograph: Paul S. Bartholomew
Designer: Naomi Stein

Appliances were the driving force in Naomi Stein's design of this kitchen. The space features a large commercial range, 48-inch refrigerator, two sinks, two dishwashers, a beverage cooler, trash compactor, and warming drawer. Because of the space requirements for these appliances, the cabinetry had to be very efficient. Almost every cabinet offers specialized storage. The island conceals three appliances and is finished with a reclaimed chestnut countertop. The turned legs ground the island and fit well with other decorative trim features in the home. The detailing of the doors and stiles was meticulously designed and executed to provide 1½-inch beaded framework between every door and at each cabinet to cabinet intersection. With no space for a traditional pantry, a narrow depth bank of armoires was fashioned in over-sanded black, with bun feet, wire mesh doors, and pleated fabric to create the feel of old cupboards. *Courtesy of Design Manifest*

Photographer: Iesha Gomillion
Designer: Jerry Weed, CKD

Craftsmanship sensibilities were appeased with this kitchen, featuring handsome Shaker-styled cabinetry, rich wood tones, and appealing simplicity. A granite slab on the center island and a generous cooktop are features to fall in love with. *Courtesy of Kitchen & Bath Studios*

Photographer: Chris Giles
Designer: Tony McCargar

Creativity was required in order to marry the client's unique rustic streak with an upscale context. Custom hardware, a chiseled edge to the granite, and the burl panels soften the formality of the dark stained cherry cabinetry. *Courtesy of Kitchen Concepts of Durango*

Photographer: Iesha Gomillion
Designer: Jerry Weed, CKD

Gold hues suffuse this contemporary kitchen. Black cabinetry underlines the ochre hues of granite, and glass tile mixes with ceramic on a backsplash underlining a stainless steel hood and rich wood-grained cabinetry.

Photographer: Iesha Gomillion
Designer: Karen Hourigan CKD
AIA: Nick Lucatelli
Builder: Denman Construction

A pretty slate floor and artful glass pendant lighting
add eye appeal to a room richly furnished in custom
cabinetry and tile. Stone backs the steel backsplash
and hood over the cooktop and range, a solid pres-
ence in a room otherwise surrounded in glass. Round-
backed bar stools mimic the arch of granite they pay
homage to, curved presences in an otherwise linear
space. *Courtesy of Kitchen & Bath Studios*

Photographer: Bob Narod
Designer: Jerry Weed, CKD

Cabinets are stacked two deep on the wall,
capped by crown molding. The effect is to
emphasize what the kitchen has in height, and
to make up storage in its lack of floor space.
Courtesy of Kitchen & Bath Studios

Country style has long since evolved beyond ging-ham and geese. Today, those who want a casual country atmosphere for their homes are highly sophisticated in their demands. Casual in no way releases the craftsman from his cares, or cuts down on his hours. Country style cabinetry today is richly embellished with beautiful mold-ings and a tasteful mix of finishes. Country style decor allows visitors to relax amidst a quiet harmony of pretty or classic elements, at once familiar in their design, but delightful upon deeper contemplation.

Photographer: Bob Narod
Designer: Fred Grenfell

Barn red walls and accents provide a harmonious mix with the blondes of oaken wood cabinetry. Colors and textures were carefully selected to make this room glow. The appliances were neatly tucked behind panels, so that the refrigerator and coffee maker have homes harmonious with the rest of the room. Basket storage under the counter adds to the sense of timelessness. Craftsmanship sensibilities were appeased with this kitchen, featuring handsome Shaker-styled cabinetry, rich wood tones, and appealing simplicity. A granite slab on the center island and a generous cooktop are features to fall in love with. *Courtesy of Kitchen & Bath Studios*

Photographer: Bob Narod
Designer: Jerry Weed, CKD

Textiles provide character and charm to this warm, wood-toned kitchen. A window seat is added allure, though you're unlikely to hurry out of the upholstered bar stools that circle the island. *Courtesy of Kitchen & Bath Studios*

Photographer: Peter Rymwid
Designer: Joe Salerno, CKD

An island and a peninsula vastly increase this
kitchen's approachability, in keeping with the
open floor plan. A wealth of white cabinetry contributes to the bright, open feeling. *Courtesy of
Ribbon and Reed Cabinetry*

Photographer: Lisa Farrar
Designer: Susan Lund, AKBD

Brilliant white enhances the open feeling in this kitchen, marrying handsome cabinetry with the perimeters, allowing the natural oak floor to set the stage. *Courtesy of Spacial Design*

Photographer: Chris Giles
Designer: Tony McCargar

When it comes to entertaining and managing thirty-plus guests, two large islands come in handy. The custom finish on knotty pine cabinetry ties in well with the Southwest location of the home, while a paint color was chosen for the center island to compliment the granite and tile as well as to diminish the mass of this central element. The large hood doubles nicely as handy storage with pull-out spice shelving on either side of the range. *Courtesy of Kitchen Concepts of Durango*

Photographer: Pete Fournier
Designer: Eileen Hafke

Two L-shaped stretches of countertop define this kitchen,
creating its sense of space within an open floor plan, and
creating lots of base-cabinetry storage so that views outside and into other rooms could be carefully preserved.
Every possible use of under-counter space was put to work,
including pullout corner drawers, in order to conserve this
open feeling. *Courtesy of Design Matters Studio*

Photographer: Taylor Photography
Designer: Laura Todd

This eat-in kitchen is just like grandma's, only much bigger, more elegant, and far more efficient. Cabinetry may have an antique appeal, but it's all modern in function and size, while appliances are professional quality, including the stacked freezer and refrigerator which are carefully concealed behind cabinetry panels. *Courtesy of Spyglass Design, Inc.*

Photographer: Travis Hendricks
Designer: Sandy Hendricks, ASID, CKD

Left:
This kitchen was designed for a single man who loves to entertain and also has limited mobility. The upscale kitchen took on a rustic theme fitting within its high desert community. The handcrafted knotty alder cabinetry with its raised panel and edge profile rises from a contrasting backdrop of hickory plank. Graduated heights in the cabinetry give the space rhythm. The Wright glass doors add a special sparkle and the walnut colored glass mosaic tile backsplash is a strong tie between the base and upper cabinetry.

Below;
This kitchen is fit for any gourmet cook and is packed with many additional features. Many of these features are considered luxury items but when mobility is compromised they become more essential. Some key items for this customer were varied height granite slab countertops, wider aisles with a five-foot turning radius, and a lowered microwave and oven along with several pullout features. *Courtesy of Ovation Design Build*

Photographer: Peter Rymwid
Designer: Peter Salerno, CMKBD

Colorful collectibles and textiles evoke the joyful atmosphere of France's rural Provence region. Brick and natural wood tones work with the sophisticated rustic aesthetic for evocative effect. A bump-out with built-in seating and an office nook are two ways in which this kitchen multi-tasks. Comfortable seating and the lively surrounds ensure that it is almost always occupied. *Courtesy of Peter Salerno, Inc.*

POST MODERN

Contemporary a decade ago required a lot of Windex™ – chrome cabinetry, stainless appliances, and sleek laminates made every surface a shiny, bright challenge. Today's contemporary aesthetic has mellowed, with designers incorporating the warmth of wood grains and tones with brushed nickel hardware to soften the straight lines of the modern decor. That's not to say contemporary isn't still packing the in-your-face impact of streamlined lines, but the feeling has muted, with color and texture to add to its appeal. So, while welcoming, you'll find that the following contemporary kitchens haven't skimped on their basic design challenge – presenting clean lines and putting function first. It's just a little more comfortable than the factory look and feel of prior days.

Photographer: Bob Narod
Designer: Jerry Weed, CKD

Stainless steel appliances are the pride of this contemporary kitchen, surrounded by the earthy tones of wood
and tile. *Courtesy of Kitchen & Bath Studios*

Photographer: Peter Rymwid
Designer: Peter Salerno, CMKBD

When not in use by caterers, this stainless steel kitchen provides the perfect place for the homeowner to reflect on a collection of guitars. *Courtesy of Peter Salerno, Inc.*

Photographer: Mary Maurey, Owner
Designer: Mary Maurey, Owner

Two tones of cabinetry furnish this combined look of traditional and contemporary kitchen with "Vanilla" painted units, creating a foil for the more showy "Espresso" stained-wood tone. Although each seems to demand attention individually, together they manage to provide an enormous amount of storage and multiple workstations, while keeping the sight lines open throughout the large space.
Courtesy of That Design Place

Photographer: Terry Roberts
Designer: Catherine Hodgins

Blonde finishes reflect a golden light in this spacious kitchen. A crescent countertop creates elevated seating capping one end of the spacious island and affording views in three directions. *Courtesy of Kitchens by Design*

Photographer: Iesha Gomillion
Designer: Jerry Weed, CKD

A coffered ceiling carries on the effect of three full-paned glass French doors that wall one side of this kitchen. A big blond island provides both food-prep service and room to sit down and eat it. Against the walls, spacious cabinetry conceal a wealth of food stock, cookware, and serving ware, preserving the room's pristine nature. *Courtesy of Kitchen & Bath Studios*

Photographer: Iesha Gomillion
Designer: Jerry Weed, CKD

The owner took a daring leap and let her designer incorporate color – lots of exciting color – into her kitchen. *Courtesy of Kitchen & Bath Studios*

Photographer: Iesha Gomillion
Designer: Karen Hourigan CKD
INEX Design Principle:
Kim Sammis

Chocolate base cabinetry
and white wall cabinets help
to add a modern sleek look
to a small kitchen. While not
sparing on the acquisition of
professional-quality appliances, they were stacked
against one wall to save
space, and share room with
stainless steel storage units
above. An inviting nook
offers bench seating close
to the action. The cabinets
next to the nook also serve
as a desk. The ceiling soffit
lighting adds class to this
Virginia suburban home.
*Courtesy of Kitchen & Bath
Studios*

Photographer: Iesha Gomillion
AIA: Richard Wieboldt
INT: S. Daniels DZYN
Designer: Karen Hourigan, CKD

A huge portion of the open floor plan in this home was dedicated to a kitchen. A wealth of professional-quality appliances adds steel glimmer to a sparkling white environment, overlooked by a bank of ceiling-level windows. An impressive hood crowns the central cooktop, and countertop seating invites onlookers from two directions. *Courtesy of Kitchen & Bath Studios*

Photographer: Pete Fournier
Designer: Eileen Hafke

A galley kitchen stretches long and tall through the heart of this home, its sleek nature emphasized by smooth cabinetry, stainless steel appliances, and space-age-styled lighting. Cushioned chairs preserve its sense of comfort. *Courtesy of Design Matters Studio*

Photographer: Chris Weskosfeske
Designer: Linda Burkhardt Kitchen & Bath

Frosted glass panels and cool earthy colors
drafted straight from the vegetable crisper
characterize this contemporary kitchen.
Courtesy of Linda Burkhardt

Photographer: Chris Weskosfeske
Designer: Linda Burkhardt

Windows take full advantage of a seafront view. Under-counter storage, including a wealth of space under the large central island, help
eliminate the need for wall cabinets. Built-in seating contributes to
the open feeling of the room. *Courtesy of Linda Burkhardt*

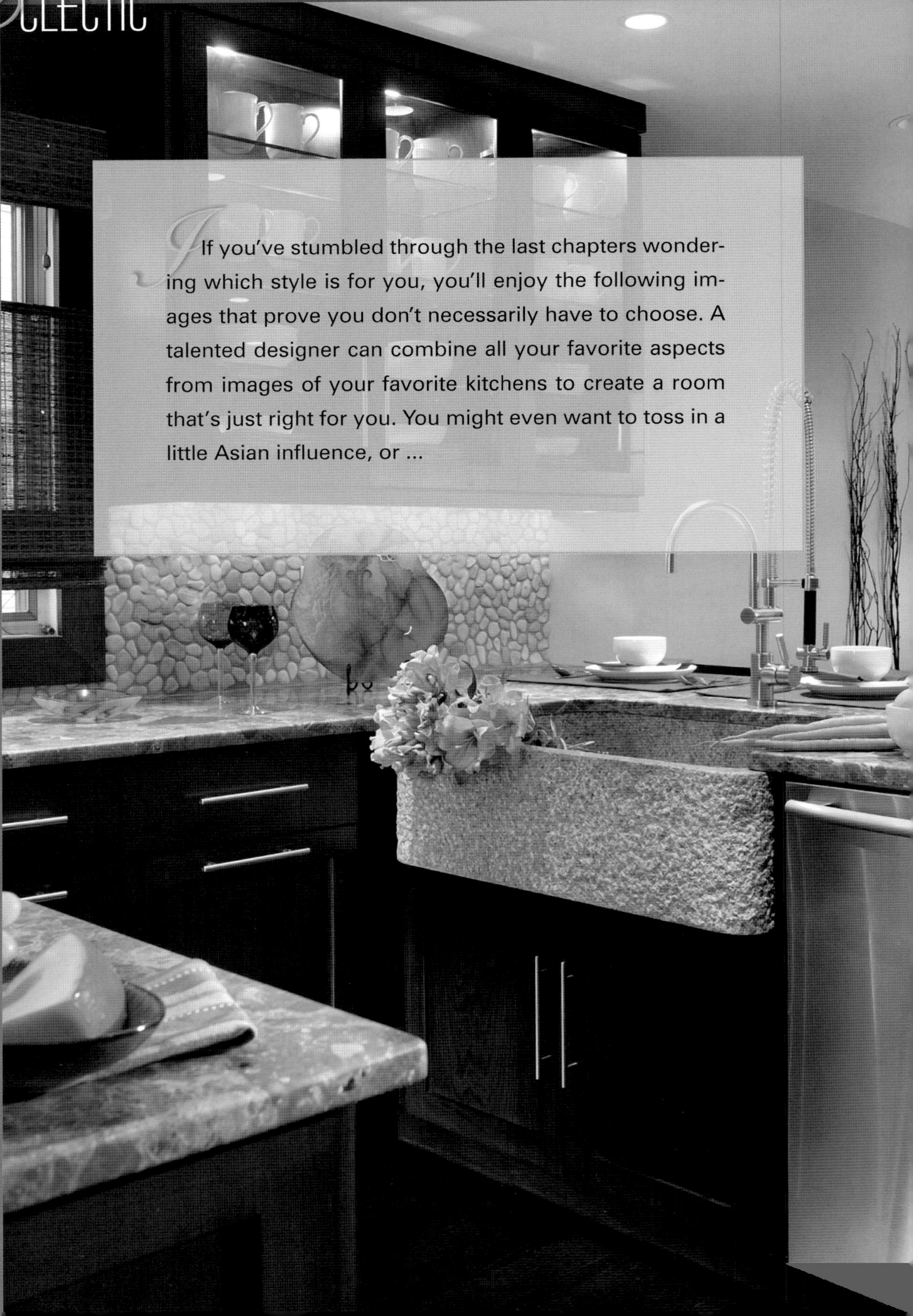

If you've stumbled through the last chapters wondering which style is for you, you'll enjoy the following images that prove you don't necessarily have to choose. A talented designer can combine all your favorite aspects from images of your favorite kitchens to create a room that's just right for you. You might even want to toss in a little Asian influence, or ...

Photographer: Peter Rymwid
Designer: Joe Salerno, CKD

Art Deco flair characterizes this central island, creating a "modern" stage for a thoroughly modern kitchen. Dark wood tones underline the bright white and stainless amenities that make this room shine. *Courtesy of Ribbon and Reed Cabinetry*

Photographer: Lisa Farrer
Designer: Susan Lund, AKBD

A stretch of kitchen features a hide-away range top, complete with five gas burners. Display cabinetry compliments the slick modern functionality of the kitchen, while warm cherry cabinetry unites the scheme with nature. *Courtesy of Spacial Design*

Photographer: Iesha Gomillion
Designer: Jerry Weed, CKD

Black cabinetry and a red-stained floor create Japanese sensibility for this modern kitchen. The cook's amenities include a spice drawer close at hand, storage drawers under the cooktop, as well as a pull-out next to the range for easy accessibility to pots and pans.
Courtesy of Kitchen & Bath Studios

Photographer: Iesha Gomillion
Designer: Fred Grenfell, CKD

Playing with circles, this kitchen gets "wow" factor from an elevated sink surround on the island and a bowed range hood. Green paint highlights the blonde of beautiful cabinetry, and re-emphasizes the owner's willingness to take risks.
Courtesy of Kitchen & Bath Studios

121

Photographer: Peter Rymwid
Designer: Peter Salerno, CMKBD

At first glance, this kitchen appears to be a two-tone masterpiece; a spacious, open white room warmed by rich wood cabinetry. Closer inspection, however, reveals a wealth of texture and detail. *Courtesy of Peter Salerno, Inc.*

Photographer: Peter Rymwid
Designer: Peter Salerno, CMKBD

The river-stone backsplash and hewn-stone textured farmer's sink are among the delightful surprises in store for a visitor to this kitchen. *Courtesy of Peter Salerno, Inc.*

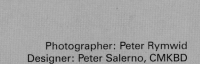

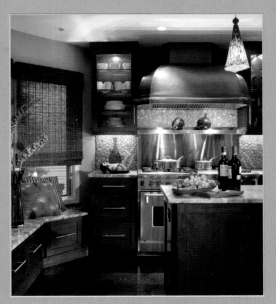

Photographer: Peter Rymwid
Designer: Peter Salerno, CMKBD

Red accessories might as easily be replaced by the next day's favorite color for a seamless transition to an alternate theme. *Courtesy of Peter Salerno, Inc.*

Photographer: Peter Rymwid
Designer: Peter Salerno, CMKBD

A built-in window seat offers storage below, great views above. White tableware is artfully stacked and illuminated in glass-front cabinetry, while copper pots and tones in glassware compliment the impressive range hood. *Courtesy of Peter Salerno, Inc.*

Photographer: Peter Rymwid
Designer: Peter Salerno, CMKBD

A three-way fireplace adds instant gas fire to both food preparation and dining areas. *Courtesy of Peter Salerno, Inc.*

123

Photography: Lydia Cutter Photography
Designer: Karen Hourigan

Grey tones, stainless steel, and richly veined white marble create the contemporary aura for this petite kitchen that packs a lot of impression. *Courtesy of Kitchen & Bath Studios*

After kitchen upgrades, bathrooms are usually the next room in an older home that demand a redo. Moreover, today's new home builders are providing what the customer wants with grand master baths that include wonderful soaking tubs, dressing areas, and even vanities, in many cases. If you're hoping to create a bath that would be the envy of royalty, the following are fine examples.

Photographer: Peter Rymwid
Designer: Joe Salerno, CKD

Cabinetry frames a his-and-hers vanity area and
provides a wealth of storage space. *Courtesy of
Ribbon and Reed Cabinetry*

Photographer: Terry Roberts
Designer: Catherine Hodgins

Bowl sinks cap a symmetrical arrangement of bathroom suite cabinetry while a mirror reflects the jet tub and glass block shower stall beyond. *Courtesy of Kitchens by Design*

Photographer: Iesha Gomillion
Designer: Jerry Weed, CKD

Asian influences are evident in a contemporary bath, with a pedestal sink mounted atop an asymmetrical assembly of contemporary cabinetry. *Courtesy of Kitchen & Bath Studios*

Photographer: Iesha Gomillion
Designer: Fred Grenfell, CKD

Dual sinks grace the rounded ends of a generous stretch of vanity, with a moon mirror front and center, and column-like storage flanking them. The effect is Art Deco, with warm wood tones. *Courtesy of Kitchen & Bath Studios*

Photographer: Paul S. Bartholomew
Designer: Naomi Stein

A large mosaic tile mandala in the middle of the bath area coordinates with the tile and marble border on the tub and shower walls. The jetted pedestal tub is the focal point of the room, flanked by the steam shower and privatized toilet area. A flat panel television fits seamlessly into the design and is viewable from tub and shower. Other features include a surround-sound stereo system, a hydronic towel warmer, and body sprays in the shower. *Courtesy of Design Manifest*

Photographer Paul Bartholomew
Designer: Naomi Stein

Designer Naomi Stein created this master suite to be a luxurious re-treat for a busy mom. The large space was divided into a master clos-et and bathroom with coordinating cabinetry and heated tile floors throughout. A domed ceiling was constructed to create an open, yet soft feel to the room, and arches and curves were used throughout the rooms to give a sense of visual continuity. The bathroom vani-ties were separated to create a space for the lavatory and a curved nook for make-up and dressing. Cabinetry provides ample storage for toiletries, linens, and two hampers, and they conceal the steam unit, tub pump, and A/V equipment.

The master closet features the same latte cabinets as the bathroom. Storage was meticulously planned to provide a balanced space for all types of shoes, clothes, and accessories. Double hanging is concealed behind armoire doors, while other items, such as shoes, are out for easy view. *Courtesy of Design Manifest*

Photographer: Taylor
Photography
Designer: Laura Todd

A master suite is
relatively small space
wise, but huge on
impact with custom
cabinetry and a to-
die-for spa surround.
*Courtesy of Spyglass
Design, Inc.*

Photographer: Beth Alongi
Designer: Julie Stoner, CKD, ASID

A master suite is furnished like a day spa, with a private soaking tub window-side, and another cushioned window seat for drier contemplation. Display cabinetry complements a glass shower, with the light and airy room united by forest green cabinetry and trim. *Courtesy of Kitchen & Bath Galleria*

Photographer: Beth Alongi
Designer: Julie Stoner, CKD, ASID

Ebony and ivory adorn a handsome guest bath.
Courtesy of Kitchen & Bath Galleria

Photographer: Beth Alongi
Designer: Julie Stoner, CKD, ASID

A dual-sink vanity celebrates the beauty of wood and stone. *Courtesy of Kitchen & Bath Galleria*

Photographer: Steven Paul Whitsitt
Designer: Interstate Custom Kitchens

A tub surround with its matching built-in shelf and the nearby custom vanity add a sense of establishment to this home spa. *Courtesy of Interstate Custom Kitchens*

Home Furnishings

Custom cabinetry can be the crowning touch in many rooms of the home, from the built-in cabinetry and fireplace surround in your living area, to the shelves and desk in your private library. The following are inspiring examples of rooms where cabinetry makes the look memorable.

Photographer: Taylor Photography
Designer: Laura Todd

A spacious den was upgraded with a coffered ceiling and built-in bookshelves and cabinetry. *Courtesy of Spyglass Design, Inc.*

Photographer: Terry Roberts

Bowl sinks cap a symmetrical arrange-ment of bathroom suite cabinetry while a mirror reflects the jet tub and glass block shower stall beyond. *Cour-tesy of Kitchens by Design*

Below:
Photographer: Chris Giles
Designer: Tony McCargar

Custom burl wood finishes the cherry door style on this entertainment unit that conceals a retract-able 72-inch flat screen television. *Courtesy of Kitchen Concepts of Durango*

Photographer: Chris Giles
Designer: Tony McCargar

This upscale, yet comfortable, home office was crafted with dark-stained cherry cabinetry to complement the flooring and stone hearth. Filing cabinets and computer components are neatly tucked out of site so the room can double as a home "getaway" while attending to important business. *Courtesy of Kitchen Concepts of Durango*

Photographer: Taylor Photography
Designer: Laura Todd

A foyer is outfitted with custom cabinetry to maximize storage for outdoor gear, as well as a coat closet fit for guest's coats. *Courtesy of Spyglass Design, Inc.*

Below:
Photographer: Taylor Photography
Designer: Laura Todd

Built-in cabinetry enhances the sense of space and freedom in this bedroom suite. *Courtesy of Spyglass Design, Inc.*

Photographer: Taylor Photography
Designer: Gayla Olson

A built-in window seat provides storage, along with a wonderful window-illuminated reading nook. *Courtesy of Spyglass Design, Inc.*

CONTRIBUTORS

Asbury Kitchen & Bath
929 Asbury Avenue
Ocean City, NJ 08226
(609) 399-6050

Brindisi Builders
59 South Maple Avenue
Marlton, NJ 08053
(856) 985-6219

Chester County Kitchen & Bath
724 E. Union Street
West Chester, PA 19382
(610) 430-3460

Claudia Harvey
27 Farrington Lane
Branchburg, NJ 08876
(908) 575-9393

Christiana Cabinetry
P. O. Box 40
Christiana, PA 17509
(610) 593-7500

Design Manifest
P. O. Box 254
5 Maple Avenue
Bala Cynwyd, PA 19004
(610) 667-7711

Design Matters Studio
12496 Water Oak Drive
Wild Cat Run
Estero, FL 33928
(239) 948-3853

Interstate Custom Kitchen & Bath
558 Chicopee Street
Chicopee, MA 01013
(413) 532-2727

Kitchen & Bath Galleria
350 Esplanade #56
Boca Raton, FL 33432
(561) 391-9501

Kitchen & Bath Studios
7001 Wisconsin Avenue
Chevy Chase, MD 20815
(301) 657-1636

Kitchens by Design
1855 Marsh Road
Wilmington, DE 19810
(302) 529-7015

Kitchen Concepts of Durango
329 S. Camino Del Rio, Suite A
Durango, CO 81303
(970) 259-9533

Kitchen DeBonaire
P. O. Box 3619
Rancho Santa Fe, CA 92067
(858) 756-6608

Kitchens & Baths, Linda Burkhardt
771 Montauk Highway, Suite 2
Montauk, NY 11954
(631) 668-6806

Ovation Design Build
17613 Kelok Road
Lake Oswego, OR 97035
(503) 635-3456

Peter Salerno, Inc.
511 Goffle Road
Wyckoff, NJ 07481
(201) 251-6608

PRO Interiors
1113 SW 47th Terrace, Unit 7
Cape Coral, FL 33904
(239) 542-2122

Ribbon & Reed Cabinetry
713 Hillcrest Road
Washington Township, NJ 07676
(201) 664-7050

Sage Kitchens
50 Franklin Hills Drive
Bozeman, MT 59715
(406) 522-0178

Spacial Design
524 San Anselmo Avenue, Suite 146
San Anselmo, CA 94960
(415) 382-1218

Spyglass Design Inc.
31 West Broad Street
Hopewell, NJ 08525
(609) 466-7900

That Design Place
P. O. Box 72
Clarksville, MD 21029
(301) 596-7799

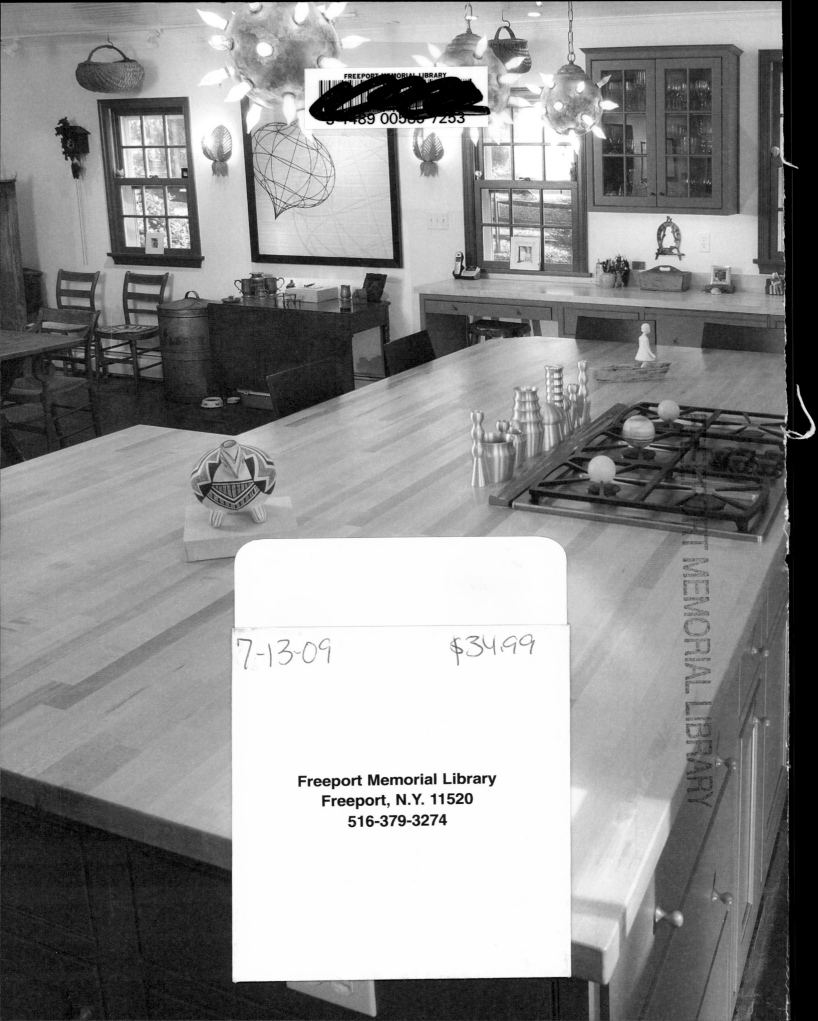

7-13-09 $34.99